How To Write Your Own Ticket With God

KENNETH E. HAGIN

Chapter 1
JESUS APPEARS TO ME

One night as some friends were preparing to serve refreshments after a service in Phoenix, Arizona, I had an unusually strong urge from the Holy Spirit to pray.

"I *have* to pray. I *must* pray. I have *got* to pray now," I told my friends.

"Let's just all pray, then," they agreed.

My knees had hardly touched the floor until I was in the Spirit. Do you know what it means to be in the Spirit? John was in the Spirit on the Lord's day (Rev. 1:10). It seemed to me like I knelt in a white cloud as I began to speak in tongues.

First the Lord showed me a detailed vision of a 72-year-old man who was going to be saved in the coming Sunday night service.

Then the Lord Jesus Himself appeared to me. I saw him as clearly as I would see you. He stood within three feet of me. He discussed things concerning my ministry and finances, and He even discussed things concerning our United States government. All of these things came to pass just as He said they would. He concluded by exhorting me, "Be faithful, and fulfill thy ministry, my son, for the time is short." This vision took place in December 1953.

Jesus turned around to walk away, and I said, "Dear Lord Jesus, before You go, may I please ask You a question?"

He retraced His steps, stood close to where I was kneeling, and said, "You may."

I said, "Dear Lord, I have two sermons I preach concerning the woman who touched Your clothes and was healed when You were on earth. I received both of these sermons by inspiration. I preach them everywhere I go. And every time I preach them, I seem to be conscious in my spirit that the Holy Spirit is trying to get another sermon from this fifth chapter of Mark to me—a sermon that would complement the first two.

"Then, at times of prayer when I have a great anointing," I said, "I will come to the place where it seems I am going to receive that message into my spirit, but somehow or other, I fail to. If I am right about this, I wish You would give me that sermon."

He said, "You are correct. My Spirit, the Holy Spirit, has endeavored to get another sermon into your spirit, but you have failed to pick it up. While I am here, I will do what you ask. I will give you that sermon outline. Now get your pencil and paper and write it down."

I opened my eyes to ask for paper and pencil. I didn't see Jesus any longer; I saw the people who were praying with me. When I closed my eyes, there Jesus stood as before. This was a spiritual vision.

There are three types of visions: (1) *a spiritual vision*, when you see with the eyes of your spirit; (2) *a trance*, when your physical senses are suspended, and you do not know, at that moment, that you have a body; and (3) what I call *an open vision*, the highest type of vision, when your physical senses are all intact. You are not in a trance. Your eyes are wide open, yet you see into the spirit realm.

I am not smart enough to have figured all of this out. One time when Jesus appeared to me in a vision, He told me there are three kinds of visions. He explained them to me and proved them with Scriptures. But you do not have to accept this just because I said so. Do not accept anything anyone tells you just because they had a vision if it cannot be proven by the Word of God.

If Jesus tells you anything—if the Spirit of God brings any revelation to you—it must be in line with the Bible, or it is not from the Spirit of God. Holy men of old wrote the Scripture as they were moved by the Holy Spirit (2 Peter 1:21), and the Holy Spirit is not going to contradict Himself, or make Himself out a liar.

Jesus said, "Write down: 1, 2, 3, 4." With my eyes shut, I wrote down 1, 2, 3, 4. I knew the sermon had four points.

He said, *"If anybody, anywhere, will take these four steps or put these four principles into operation, he will always receive whatever he wants from Me or from God the Father."*

I need to explain here that these four steps He gave me can be put into operation immediately, and you can receive anything in the present tense, such as salvation, the baptism of the Holy Spirit, healing for your body, spiritual victory, or finances. Anything that the Bible promises you now, you can receive now by taking these four steps.

However, some things, such as some financial needs and the manifestation of some healings, etc., may take time to develop. Then the four steps become principles that you must put into practice over a period of time. (A farmer cannot go out tomorrow and start picking cotton or thrashing wheat until it has had time to grow.) But, thank God, whether they are steps to be taken immediately, or principles to be practiced over time, you can have what you say.

You can write your own ticket with God. Jesus said, "Step 1: Say it."

It is so simple it almost seems foolish. Every one of the four steps is simple. After all, Jesus, in all of His preaching, never brought out anything very complicated. Did you ever notice that? He talked in terms that even the uneducated could understand, because few of the people He preached to had the advantage of an education.

Jesus talked about vineyards and orchards, sheepfolds and shepherds. He illustrated spiritual verities in such a simple way that the common people could understand Him. God never gives anybody anything so complicated that it cannot be understood. If it comes from the Father, it will be clear, concise, and simple.

We think sometimes that Jesus always initiated healings on His own; that the people had nothing to do with it. We may not stop to think that the people then, as now, had something to do with it; they had their part to play. What if the blind man had not washed the clay off his eyes in the pool of Siloam (John 9)? Would he have seen? No, he would not have seen. What about the man lying by the pool of Bethesda (John 5)? What if he had said, "I can't get up!" Did he have any part to play? Yes, he did!

Jesus asked me this question: "What was the first step the woman with the issue of blood took toward receiving her healing?"

The Bible says that someone had told her about Jesus (Mark 5:27). She knew about Jesus. She knew He was healing people. The 28th verse tells us, *"For **she said**, If I may touch but his clothes, I shall be whole."* That is the first thing she did: *She said.*

In my vision, Jesus said, "Positive or negative, it is up to the individual. According to what the individual says, that shall he receive."

He said, "This woman could have made a negative confession instead of a positive one, and that would have been what she received. She could have said, 'There's no use for me to go. I've suffered so long. Twelve years I've been sick. All the best doctors have given up on my case. I've spent all of my living upon physicians. I'm not better, but growing worse. I have nothing to live for. I might as well die.' "

He said, "If that had been what she said, that would have been what she received. But she did not speak negatively. She spoke positively. For she said, 'If I may touch but his clothes, I shall be whole.' " And it came to pass!

For you can have what you say. ***You can write your own ticket with God.*** And the first step in writing your own ticket with God is: *Say it.*

Chapter 2
YOUR VICTORIOUS CONFESSION

You see, there are two parts to everything you receive from God: the part God plays and the part you play. God is not going to fail in doing His part. You know that. If you do your part, you can be sure of an answer and the victory.

Now, if you are defeated, you are defeated with your own lips. You have defeated yourself. The Bible says in Proverbs 6:2, *"Thou art snared with the words of thy mouth."* (Or, "Thou art taken captive with the words of thy mouth.")

One writer put it this way: "You said that you could not, and the moment you said it, you were whipped. You said that you did not have faith, and doubt rose up like a giant, and bound you. You talked failure, and failure held you in bondage."

If you talk about your trials, your difficulties, your lack of faith, your lack of money—your faith will shrivel and dry up. But, bless God, if you talk about the Word of God, your lovely Heavenly Father and what He can do—your faith will grow by leaps and bounds.

If you confess sickness, it will develop sickness in your system. If you talk about your doubts and fears, they will grow and become stronger. If you confess lack of finances, it will stop the money from coming in. Although that may sound like a paradox, it is not. It is the truth. I have proven it true again and again.

Chapter 3
ACCORDING TO YOUR ACTIONS

Step 2: Do it.

Jesus dictated to me during my vision, "Your action defeats you or puts you over. According to your action, you receive or you are kept from receiving."

That is important! Let me state it again: Your action defeats you or puts you over. According to your action, you receive or you are kept from receiving.

This woman in Mark 5 had a number of obstacles to overcome. She did not pray that God would remove the obstacles; she just got up and walked over the top of them.

A woman with an issue of blood was regarded in the same category as a leper and was not to mix in public, according to the teaching of her religion. But her actions said,

"Religion or no religion, I'm going to get my healing."

In that day, women did not have the privilege to mingle publicly. But again her actions said, "Custom or no custom, I'm going to get my healing."

When she got there, a multitude of people crowded between her and Jesus. In her weakened physical condition, that would have been enough to cause her to give up. But, blessed be God, her actions said, "Crowd or no crowd, I'm getting to Jesus," and she elbowed her way through.

This woman's actions showed her faith. Now get up and walk on top of the obstacles that have been standing between you and Jesus, and you and healing. Put *actions* as well as words with your faith.

It would not have done the woman with the issue of blood any good to have said, *"If I may touch but his clothes"* (v. 28) if she had not *acted* on what she said. She *did* it, praise God, and she received.

Step 3: Receive it.

Say it. Do it. Receive it.

"She felt in her body that she was healed of

that plague" (v. 29).

Jesus said, "Virtue has gone out of me. Somebody has touched me" (v. 30). (Or as a marginal note reads, "He said, Power has gone out of me.")

I want you to notice something. Notice that the *feeling* and the *healing* followed the *coming* and the *doing*.

The woman *said* it first. She *came* for it second. Then she *received,* and *felt* in her body that she was healed. Most people want the feeling and the healing first, before the saying and doing, but that's not how it works. You have to have the saying and action first. Then you will have the healing and feeling.

Jesus said, "Power has gone out of me." At that time, Jesus was the only representative of the Godhead at work on earth. He was anointed by the Holy Spirit. When He was on earth, if you wanted to go where the power was, you had to go where He was.

In Luke 5:17, the Bible says He was teaching on a certain day, and the Pharisees and doctors of the law from every town in Galilee and Judea were gathered to hear him. *"And the power of the Lord was present to heal*

14

them."

Jesus delegated a certain amount of that power to the 12 and sent them out, and He delegated a certain amount to the 70 and sent them out. Then, before He went away, He said, *"It is expedient for you that I go away: for if I go not away, the Comforter will not come unto you"* (John 16:7).

When Jesus returned to heaven, He sent the third person of the Godhead, the Holy Spirit, to this earth. The Holy Spirit is the only person of the Godhead at work on the earth today.

Now, as Jesus said to me, *"Power is always present everywhere."*

Oh, if people could only realize that! He is *everywhere!*

And wherever He is, there is power.

The whole world is concerned about radioactive material that is released when nuclear bombs are exploded in the atmosphere. This is a power that cannot be seen or felt, yet it is a power that is deadly and dangerous.

There is a power at work on the earth today that is neither deadly nor dangerous—a good power, a power that heals, delivers, and sets free. And this unseen, unheard power—this supernatural power—is always present everywhere.

It is like plugging into an electrical outlet. If we can learn how to plug into this supernatural power, we can put it to work for us, and we can be healed. If every sick person in every sick room in the world just knew about this power and how to tap into it, it would heal them of every disease.

If people in institutions only knew it, there is power right there in that room where they are: more than enough power to heal them, to cure the insane, to drive out demons, and to deliver those who are bound.

If the power is there, you will ask, why isn't everyone healed? Let's return to this crowd where the sick woman pushed her way to Jesus.

"Daughter," Jesus said, *"thy faith hath made thee whole"* (v. 34). There is a secret here. It was *her faith* that caused that power to flow out to her. Jesus said to me, *"Power is always present everywhere."* Power to deliver from every sickness; power to deliver from every demon and everything that hurts or destroys. *Faith* gives it action. Now we know the secret. It is not a hidden secret. It may be a secret to some,

but it has been revealed to us and to all who will listen.

Jesus said, "Who touched me?" (v. 30), and the disciples replied, *"Thou seest the multitude thronging thee, and sayest thou, Who touched me?"* (v. 31).

Many people touched Jesus that day; some through curiosity, some accidentally, and some to see if something would happen. But no power flowed until there came a touch of faith! The minute there was a touch of faith, the power flowed out.

That day in 1934 when healing power enveloped my body and every symptom of distress, deficiency and physical wrongness was driven out of my body, I didn't realize what I was doing. I know now. I simply acted on Mark 11:23,24. I began to say, "I believe God. I believe I receive healing for the deformed heart. I believe I receive healing for the paralysis. I believe I receive healing for the incurable blood disease." Those were the only three things the doctors had told me. In case I missed something, I said, "I believe I receive healing from the top of my head to the soles of my feet."

I knew I was acting on those Scriptures, and

that is faith. Faith is acting on God's Word. Glory to God, I plugged into the power hose of heaven. I felt a warm glow strike me on the top of my head and ooze down over my body like somebody above me was pouring honey on me. It oozed over my head, down over my shoulders, down my arms, out to the ends of my fingers, and down my body. Feeling returned to the upper part of my body, where I had had perhaps 75 percent feeling. From my waist down, I felt nothing; I was dead. But when this power went down my body and out the ends of my toes, feeling returned, the paralysis disappeared and I found myself standing in the middle of the room with my hands uplifted, praising God. I'm still healed after more than 55 years.

Do you think God sent that healing power from heaven just that day? No! That power was in that room every day of those 16 months I was bedfast. Why didn't it do something? Because I hadn't turned the switch of faith on.

Many have died waiting for healing to come to them, saying, "I believe God is going to heal me *sometime.*" That is an unscriptural statement and contains no faith. It will not work.

People say, "Brother Hagin, do you know

why the Lord won't heal me?"

Sometimes I shock them by replying, "God has already done all He is ever going to do about healing you."

Their eyes get big. "You mean He's *not* going to heal me?"

I tell them, "I didn't say that. I said that He has done all He is ever going to do about healing you. You see, He sent Jesus to earth nearly 2,000 years ago, and He laid your sickness and your disease on Jesus, and Jesus bore them away. *'Himself took our infirmities, and bare our sicknesses'* (Matt. 8:17). God already has done something about your sicknesses. Why won't you accept what He has done?"

God is not *going* to do anything about it, because He already *has done* something about it. He has done something about salvation, the Holy Spirit, healing, and deliverance from demons. It is now up to you to plug in.

Faith is the plug, praise God. Just plug in.

How do you plug in?

Say it. Do it. Receive it.

Chapter 4
WRITING YOUR TICKET OF VICTORY

Step 4: Tell it.

She came and fell down before him, and *told* him all the truth" (v. 33).

Not only Jesus, but the whole crowd, heard her. She *told* Him everything she had done.

Jesus said to me, *"Tell it so others may believe."*

You see, there is a difference between the first step (she *said* what she believed would happen) and the last step (she *told* what had happened).

Yes, it is scriptural to go tell it (Mark 5:19). Praise the Lord, He didn't say, "Go and debate the question of whether a person in your condition could be healed or not." He just said, "Go tell it."

In the vision, I said, "Lord, I can see that. I

can see if anybody would take these four steps, they would receive healing just like that woman did.

"But now You said if anybody anywhere would take those four steps, they would receive from You *whatever they wanted*. Do You mean that people can receive the infilling of the Holy Spirit that way?"

He said, "Most assuredly, yes."

Then I said to Him, "Lord, what about Christians? So many believers need victory in various areas of their life. They have the world, the flesh, and the devil to deal with. Some need victory over the flesh. Some need victory over the devil. Some need victory over the world. And some need victory over all of it. Are You telling me that any believer anywhere can write a ticket of victory over the world, the flesh, and the devil? *They* can do it?"

He said emphatically, "Yes!"

He continued, "If they don't do it, it won't be done. It would be a waste of their time to pray for Me to give them the victory. They have to write their own ticket."

"But, Lord," I said, "You're going to have to give me some Scripture to prove it. Your Word says, '*In the mouth of two or three witnesses every word may be established*' (Matt. 18:16). So give me more Scripture having these same four principles in it, and I will believe it. I would not accept any vision, even if I did see You, if You could not prove what You said by the Bible."

No, He didn't reprimand me. He smiled and said, "All right."

"There is a story from the Old Testament," He said, "that you have known since you were a Sunday School boy."

I couldn't think of any story that had these four principles in it. I said, "You will have to tell me where it is."

He said, "In First Samuel, the 17th chapter, the story of David and Goliath."

"Now wait a minute," I said. "You're not going to tell me that is what David did?"

He said, "Exactly. Those are the four steps he took. The very first thing David did was *he said*" (v. 32).

You can read it for yourself. I read it after my vision. Five times David *said it* before he acted upon it.

David was sent by his father to take provisions to his brothers in the army and to find out how the war was progressing. When he got there, David found the Philistines encamped on one side of the valley, and the Israelites encamped on the other.

While David was there, a giant by the name of Goliath came out and challenged the armies of Israel, saying, "Send a man out against me. If I defeat him, you will be our servants, and if he defeats me, we will be your servants."

Not a man in Israel would go out against him; not even King Saul, who was head and shoulders taller than any man in Israel.

1 SAMUEL 17:32
32 AND DAVID SAID to Saul, Let no man's heart fail because of him; thy servant will go and fight with this Philistine.

And David said! Praise God, that's the first thing David did.

Here's a country boy, a teenager, who says he will go out and fight against the giant. His oldest brother, Eliab, had poked a little fun at his coming to the battlefield, saying, "Where are those sheep you're supposed to be watching?" Yet *David said:*

1 SAMUEL 17:34-37

34 AND DAVID SAID unto Saul, Thy servant
kept his father's sheep, and there came a lion,
and a bear, and took a lamb out of the flock:

35 And I went out after him, and smote him, and
delivered it out of his mouth: and when he arose
against me, I caught him by his beard, and smote
him, and slew him.

36 Thy servant slew both the lion and the bear:
and this uncircumcised Philistine shall be as one
of them, seeing he hath defied the armies of the
living God.

37 DAVID SAID MOREOVER, The Lord that
delivered me out of the paw of the lion, and out of
the paw of the bear, he will deliver me out of the
hand of this Philistine.

David knew you can have what you say. He
knew **you can write your own ticket**. He is
writing it here. He knew God would do anything he would believe Him for. God will do the
same for you, too. The only reason He has not
done more for you is because you have not
believed Him for more.

In fact, **all you are and all you have today
is the result of what you believed and said
in the past.**

Someone told Saul what David had said. He sent for him.

Saul wanted to give David his armor, but David wouldn't take it. *"And David said unto Saul, I cannot go with these; for I have not proved them"* (v. 39).

David went out against Goliath armed only with his shepherd's sling and staff. When the giant saw him, he disdained David "for he was but a youth, and ruddy." Goliath said, "Am I a dog, that thou comest to me with staves?"

Goliath cursed David by his heathen gods and threatened him. David let him talk. You can't stop the devil from talking. Let him blab. But when he gets through, you have something to say.

AND DAVID SAID (he's still writing that ticket), *"Thou comest to me with a sword, and with a spear, and with a shield: but I come to thee in the name of the Lord of hosts, the God of the armies of Israel, whom thou hast defied"* (v. 45).

David is not through yet! David told Goliath, "I will feed your carcass and the carcasses of the host of the Philistines this day unto the fowls of the air, and to the wild beasts of the earth."

How could a teenage country boy say that? He was not a soldier. He had never been trained to fight. Yet here he is confronting a giant.

How tall was this giant? I did a little research. The Bible tells us that Goliath was six cubits and a span in height. According to the famous Jewish historian, Flavius Josephus, a cubit was measured differently at different times in Israel's history. If measured by the shorter length, Goliath was almost 10 feet tall. If measured by the longer length, Goliath was about 11 feet tall.

What did David do? David did not look at the situation from the standpoint of "how big I am" or "what I can do from the natural standpoint." He looked at it from the standpoint of "my God can do it."

David was measuring the giant by the size of God. It did not matter if Goliath were 11 feet tall. Compared to God, there is not even the resemblance of an ant to an elephant—not even the tiniest ant.

When you begin to measure your problems like this, your situation looks different. You see, "giants" look big when we measure ourselves by them.

You may be facing some of them today. I've faced them through the years. But when you put them beside God, they don't look big at all. Because He's bigger. He's Bigger. He's BIGGER. He's GREATER! Greater is He that is in you than he that is in the world (1 John 4:4). Let's think in line with God's Word.

God is greater than the devil. He's greater than the giants that are in the land. He's greater than the enemy we face. He's greater than any power that can come against us. He's greater than any force that can be unleashed upon us.

When you think like that, when you look at things like that, when you believe and talk like that, sooner or later, you're going to arrive. David ran and hastened to meet the giant. He cut off the giant's head.

First, David *said* it. Second, he *did* it. Third, he *received* it. And fourth, they *told* it. The women got their tambourines and musical instruments and began to dance and sing, *"Saul has slain his thousands, but David his ten thousands"* (1 Sam. 18:7).

Some might wonder, "Well, how did David know what God would do?"

Well, He will do everything He said He would do, and He will do everything you believe Him for. **You can write your own ticket.**

Are you ready to write your ticket? If you need healing or victory over the world, the flesh, or the devil, say and act on God's Word, "I am writing a ticket of victory today."

You don't even have to have hands laid on you for healing.

People bound by habits like tobacco and dope have stood in front of me and said, "Brother Hagin, that thing left me, and I don't want it anymore." They wrote a ticket of victory. They said, "I've never been bothered by demons anymore." They took that giant's head off.

Don't measure yourself by the giant. Measure the giant by God.

Jesus said to me, "Israel is a type of the people of God. Goliath can be any giant that might be in your life: a type of the devil, demons, the world, the flesh, sickness, or anything else that stands between God's people and victory. Every child of God can write a ticket of victory."

Chapter 5
LIVING THE LIFE OF VICTORY

In 1952, we were planning to hold a tent meeting in Clovis, New Mexico. When I told my mother about our proposed trip, she told me to drive carefully because "there are so many wrecks all the time."

She admitted that when I traveled, she stayed awake all night, praying, afraid a call would come saying I had been in a wreck. I told her that if she had been praying in faith, she could have gone to sleep. (I had to tell my own mother the truth just the same as anyone else.)

She said, "Son, I know you have faith. I never had much myself." (She was a member of a Full Gospel Church, too, and she was talking herself right out of God's blessings.)

She said she knew I probably prayed every minute I was on the road.

I told her, "I never do. I never even pray that God will be with me."

"What makes you talk that way? What's gotten into you?" she said.

"Nothing but the Word," I told her. I reminded her that Jesus had already promised us, *"I will never leave thee nor forsake thee"* (Heb. 13:5). I told her I always start out by saying, "Heavenly Father, I'm so thankful for Your Word. I am so glad Jesus is with me."

The 34th Psalm says, *"The angel of the Lord encampeth round about them that fear him, and delivereth them."* I told my mother that angels, as well as God, Jesus, and the Holy Spirit, are with me. I go singing and rejoicing.

Writing your own ticket with God, however, does not mean that things will fall on you like ripe cherries from a tree. You are not going to float through life on flowery beds of ease. The devil will try you and tempt you.

In 1954, after holding meetings in Oregon, we stopped in Salt Lake City to see the great Mormon Temple on the way home. As non-Mormons, we could not go inside, but a guide told us about the interior. He explained how the Mormons transported the stones by ox cart and built the temple to last for eternity.

On the spire of the temple is the likeness of an angel blowing a trumpet. This statue, of copper overlaid with gold leaf, is 12½ feet high. It is supposed to be the angel Moroni, who supposedly appeared to Joseph Smith in the 1820s and told him to dig up the gold plates from which Smith said he translated the Book of Mormon.

I cannot accept the Book of Mormon. I have read it, but it does not agree with the New Testament. As the Apostle Paul said, *"But though we, or an angel from heaven, preach any other gospel unto you than that which we have preached unto you, let him be accursed"* (Gal. 1:8).

As we stood there on the lawn listening to the guide, I heard someone behind me fall so hard his head popped up and hit again. A man said that a boy had fallen. The guide said, "That happens very often when I'm telling this story." He thought it was a supernatural sign to corroborate what he was telling. He said to drag the boy back around the tree; he would come to in a minute.

I did not look back, but my wife did, and she

said it was our son, Ken Jr., who was 15 years old at the time. He had hit the ground so hard that his shoes were kicked off. His knees were drawn right up to his chest. His hands were twisted, and his mouth was working in such convulsions that he was chewing his tongue. His eyes were set and glazed.

Faster than machine gun bullets can fly, the devil shot his darts into my mind and said, "You said that that couldn't happen to your child." He gave me mental visions of my son having epilepsy or some other kind of disease and being in an institution while I was out preaching.

But, thank God, I knew how to write my ticket with God.

I grabbed my son by the arms to lift him up. He was stiff. I said, "Come out of him!" I had sensed evil spirits when I walked on those grounds. I said, "I command you to come out of him in the Name of the Lord Jesus Christ!"

Ken straightened out and blinked his eyes. He called to me, and asked where he was and what had happened to him. I told him that the devil had knocked him down, but that Jesus was bigger than the devil. We wrote our own ticket of victory.

The guide had said it was a supernatural manifestation verifying what he had said, but I got rid of his manifestation with the name of Jesus. You can say it and do it.

You have authority over the devil. You don't need to be defeated.

You can write your own ticket with God.

1. Say it.
2. Do it.
3. Receive it.
4. Tell it.

A Sinner's Prayer
To Receive Jesus as Savior

Dear Heavenly Father,
I come to You in the Name of Jesus.
Your Word says, "... *him that cometh to me I will in
no wise cast out*" (John 6:37).
So I know You won't cast me out,
   but You take me in.
And I thank You for it.

You said in Your Word, "... *if thou shalt confess with
thy mouth the Lord Jesus, and shalt believe
in thine heart that God hath raised him
from the dead, THOU SHALT BE SAVED....
For whosoever shall call upon the name
of the Lord shall be saved*" (Rom. 10:9,13).
I believe in my heart that Jesus Christ is the Son of God.
I believe He was raised from the dead for my
   justification.
I am calling upon His Name — the Name of Jesus —
   so I know, Father, that You save me now.

Your Word says, "... *with the heart man
believeth unto righteousness; and with the mouth
confession is made unto salvation*" (Rom. 10:10).
I do believe with my heart, and I confess Jesus now as my Lord.
Therefore I am saved!
Thank You, Father!

Signed   _____

Date   _____

About the Author

The ministry of Kenneth E. Hagin has spanned more than 60 years since God miraculously healed him of a deformed heart and incurable blood disease at the age of 17. Today the scope of Kenneth Hagin Ministries is worldwide. The ministry's radio program, "Faith Seminar of the Air," is heard coast-to-coast in the U.S., and reaches more than 100 nations. Other outreaches include: *The Word of Faith*, a free monthly magazine; crusades, conducted nationwide; RHEMA Correspondence Bible School; RHEMA Bible Training Center; RHEMA Alumni Association and RHEMA Ministerial Association International; and a prison ministry outreach.

Kenneth Hagin Ministries

ISBN 0-89276-055-9